PUFFIN POETRY

80 Poems

Roger McGough was born in Liverpool, and received the Freedom of the City in 2001. President of the Poetry Society, he presents the popular Radio 4 programme *Poetry Please*, and has published many books for adults and children. In 2005 he received a CBE from the Queen for his services to literature.

www.rogermcgough.org.uk

Books by Roger McGough

For children
SKY IN THE PIE
PILLOW TALK
BAD BAD CATS
THE BEE'S KNEES
SLAPSTICK
ALL THE BEST
LUCKY
AN IMAGINARY MENAGERIE
UNTIL I MET DUDLEY
DOTTY INVENTIONS
I NEVER LIKED WEDNESDAYS
IF ONLY WE HAD A HELICOPTER
YOU TELL ME (with Michael Rosen)

For adults
IT NEVER RAINS
AS FAR AS I KNOW
THAT AWKWARD AGE
EVERYDAY ECLIPSES
COLLECTED POEMS
SELECTED POEMS
THE MERSEY SOUND (with Adrian Henri and Brian Patten)
SUMMER WITH MONIKA

Theatre
TARTUFFE
THE HYPOCHONDRIAC
THE MISANTHROPE

Autobiography
SAID AND DONE

ROGER McGOUGH

80

Poems

Illustrated by Roger McGough

PUFFIN POETRY

PUFFIN BOOKS

UK | USA | Canada | Ireland | Australia
India | New Zealand | South Africa

Puffin Books is part of the Penguin Random House group of companies
whose addresses can be found at global.penguinrandomhouse.com.

www.penguin.co.uk
www.puffin.co.uk
www.ladybird.co.uk

First published 2017
001

Set in 13/16 pt Baskerville MT Std
Typeset by Jouve (UK), Milton Keynes
Printed in Great Britain by Clays Ltd, St Ives plc

A CIP catalogue record for this book is available from the British Library

ISBN: 978-0-141-38882-3

All correspondence to:
Puffin Books
Penguin Random House Children's
80 Strand, London WC2R ORL

MIX
Paper from
responsible sources
FSC
www.fsc.org   FSC® C018179

Penguin Random House is committed to a
sustainable future for our business, our readers
and our planet. This book is made from Forest
Stewardship Council® certified paper.

Contents

The Power of Poets

The man on the settee
stroking a cat and watching TV
isn't me.
I am the settee.

I could have been the man,
the cat or the TV.
However, this is my poem
and I choose to be the settee.
Such is the power of poets.

The Reader of This Poem

The reader of this poem
Is as cracked as a cup
As floppy as a flip-flop
As mucky as a pup

As troublesome as bubblegum
As brash as a brush
As bouncy as a double-tum
As quiet as a sshhh . . .

As sneaky as a witch's spell
As tappy-toe as jazz
As empty as a wishing-well
As echoey as as as as as as . . . as . . . as . . .

As bossy as a whistle
As prickly as a pair
Of boots made out of thistles
And elephant hair

As vain as trainers
As boring as a draw
As smelly as a drain is
Outside the kitchen door

As hungry as a wave
That feeds upon the coast
As gaping as the grave
As GOTCHA! as a ghost

As fruitless as a cake of soap
As creeping-up as smoke
The reader of this poem, I hope,
Knows how to take a joke!

Bad Jokes

What becomes of jokes that nobody laughs at?

Do they curl up in embarrassment
and wish they'd never been born?
Wish they could bite the tongue
off the one who'd made them?

Do they dread ending up
inside Christmas crackers
or in politicians' speeches?

Is a joke that nobody laughs at . . .
A bellyflop out of water?
A non-slip banana skin?
A custard pie left out in the rain?
An Englishman, an Irishman and a Scotsman
helping a chicken across the road.

Or . . .

Do jokes that nobody laughs at feel superior?
Think the joke is on us and giggle quietly among
    themselves?

Apostrophe

How nice to be
an apostrophe
floating
above an *s*

hovering
like a paper kite
in between the *it's*

eavesdropping
tiptoeing
high above the *that's*

an inky comet
spiralling
the highest-tossed
of hats.

In Case of Fire

In case of fire break glass

In case of glass fill with water

In case of water fetch umbrella

In case of umbrella beware of Mary Poppins

In case of Mary Poppins switch off TV

In case of TV change channel

In case of Channel swim across

In case of cross say sorry

In case of sorry hold out arms

In case of arms lay down gun

In case of gun *Fire*

In case of fire break glass

Cautionary Tale

A little girl called Josephine
Was fair of face and reasonably clean
But at school she wore a dunce's cap
And her father, taking out a map

Said: 'She'll learn more if she comes with me
About the world and life at sea.
What she needs is a trip on my schooner
I'm surprised I didn't think of it sooner.

For I am captain of the *Hesperus*
And I think I know what's best for us.'
And thereupon a most dreadful fate
Befell her, which I'll now relate.

It was winter when they left the port
(in retrospect they shouldn't ought)
Setting sail for the Spanish Main
Despite warnings of a hurricane.

Three days out there came the gale
Even the skipper he turned pale
And as for little Josephine
She turned seven shades of green.

As the schooner rocked from port to starboard
Across the decks poor Josie scarpered
She ran from the fo'c'sle to the stern
(Some folks'll never learn)

Crying: 'Stop the boat, I want to go home.'
But unheeding, the angry foam
Swamped the decks. Her dad did curse
Knowing things would go from bad to worse.

He pulled his daughter to his side
'Put on my seaman's coat,' he cried
'You'll be safe 'til the storm has passed.'
Then bound her tightly to the mast.

And pass it did, but sad to say
Not for a fortnight and a day.
By then the ship had foundered
And all the crew had drownded.

And reported later in the press
Was a story that caused much distress
Of a couple walking on the shore
And of the dreadful sight they saw

Tied to a mast, a few bones picked clean
All that remained of poor Josephine.

MORAL
Stay on at school, get your GCSEs
Let others sail the seven seas.

The Colour Collector

A stranger called this morning
Dressed all in black and grey
Put every colour into a bag
And carried them away

The goldenness of cornflakes
The ivory of milk
The silverness of soup spoons
The see-throughness of silk

The greenness of tennis courts
When play has just begun
The orangeness of oranges
Glowing in the sun

The blueness of a dolphin
Nosing through the sea
The redness of the breast
A robin nestling in a tree

The creaminess of polar bears
Sliding on the floes
The little piggy pinkness
Of tiny, tickly toes

The sky that smiled a rainbow
Now wears a leaden frown
Who's sobbing in his caravan?
Wizzo the monochrome clown

A stranger called this morning
He didn't leave his name
We live now in the shadows
Life will never be the same.

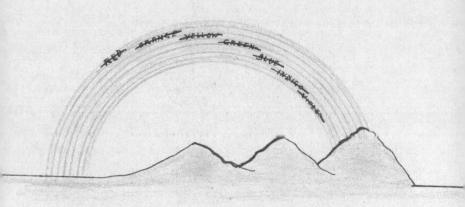

I'm a Grown Man Now

I'm a grown man now
Don't easily scare
(if you don't believe me
ask my teddy bear).

The Perfect Present

What I wanted at the age of ONE
Was a rattle to shake and chew upon

What I got at the age of 1
Was a brick with RATTLE painted on

What I wanted at the age of TWO
Was a teddy bear, faithful and true

What I got at the age of 2
Was a piece of fur and a stick of glue

What I wanted at the age of THREE
Was a tricycle as new as can be

What I got at the age of 3
Was a pair of pram wheels nailed to a tree

What I wanted at the age of FOUR
Was a fearsome, gruesome dinosaur

What I got at the age of 4
Was a plastic lobster with only one claw

What I wanted at the age of FIVE
Was a silver kite to swoop and dive

What I got at the age of 5
Was a homeless pigeon more dead than alive

What I wanted at the age of SIX
Was a magic wand and a box of tricks

What I got at the age of 6
Was a pair of granny's walking sticks

What I wanted at the age of SEVEN
Was a racing car, battery driven

What I got at the age of 7
Was a beer mat from a pub in Devon

What I wanted at the age of EIGHT
Was a surfboard, wouldn't that be great?

What I got at the age of 8
Was a swimming ring that wouldn't inflate

What I wanted at the age of NINE
Was a fishing rod with reel and line

What I got at the age of 9
Was a safety pin and a ball of twine

What I wanted at the age of TEN
Was a diary and a fountain pen

At the age of 10
Dad won the lottery. Bought me Disneyland.

Sky in the Pie!

Waiter, there's a sky in my pie
Remove it at once if you please
You can keep your incredible sunsets
I ordered mincemeat and cheese

I can't stand nightingales singing
Or clouds all burnished with gold
The whispering breeze is disturbing the peas
And making my chips go all cold

I don't care if the chef is an artist
Whose canvases hang in the Tate
I want two veg and puff pastry
Not the Universe heaped on my plate

OK I'll try just a spoonful
I suppose I've got nothing to lose
Mm . . . the colours quite tickle the palette
With a blend of delicate hues

The sun has a custardy flavour
And the clouds are as light as air
And the wind a chewier texture
(With a hint of cinnamon there?)

The sky is simply delicious
Why haven't I tried it before?
I can chew my way through to Eternity
And still have room left for more

Having acquired a taste for the Cosmos
I'll polish this sunset off soon
I can't wait to tuck into the night sky
Waiter! Please bring me the Moon!

Mrs Moon

Mrs Moon
sitting up in the sky
little old lady
rock-a-bye
with a ball of fading light
and silvery needles
knitting the night

Snuggles

Work done
for the day
the sun
switches on
the moon
pulls
the clouds
over its
head and
snuggles
right down
into the
cosy bottom
of the sky.

Pillow Talk

Last night I heard my pillow talk
What amazing things it said
About the fun that pillows have
Before it's time for bed

The bedroom is their playground
A magical place to be
(Not a room for peace and quiet
Like it is for you and me)

They divebomb off the wardrobe
Do backflips off the chair
Use the mattress as a trampoline
Turn somersaults in the air

It's Leapfrog then Pass the Slipper
Handstands and cartwheels all round
Wrestling and swinging on curtains
And all with hardly a sound

But by and by the feathers fly
And they get out of puff
So with scarves and ties they bind their eyes
For a game of Blind Man's Buff

They tiptoe out on the landing
Although it's a dangerous place
(If granny met one on the stairs
Imagine the look on her face!)

It's pillows who open cupboard drawers
To mess and rummage about
(And *you* end up by getting blamed
For something *they* left out)

I'd quite fancy being a pillow
Playing games and lying in bed
If I didn't have to spend each night
Under your big snoring head!

The Hair Fairy

I'm going bald
And it's not fair
Where, oh where
Is the Fairy of Hair?

When I was young
And a tooth fell out
You didn't hear me
Weep or shout

For the Tooth Fairy
Would come to my aid
When fast asleep
I'd be well paid

If I got a pound
For each fallen hair
By now I'd be
A millionaire.

Wouldn't It Be Funny If You Didn't Have a Nose?

You couldn't smell your dinner
If you didn't have a nose
You couldn't tell a dirty nappy
From a summer rose
You couldn't smell the ocean
Or the traffic, I suppose
Oh wouldn't it be funny
If you didn't have a nose?

You couldn't smell your mummy
If you didn't have a nose
You couldn't tell an orange
From a row of smelly toes
You couldn't smell the burning
(think how quick a fire grows)
Wouldn't it be funny
If you didn't have a nose?

Where would we be without our hooters?
Nothing else would really suit us.
What would we sniff through?
How would we sneeze?
What would we wipe
Upon our sleeves?

You couldn't smell a rat
If you didn't have a nose
You couldn't tell a duchess
From a herd of buffaloes
And . . . mmmm that Gorgonzola
As it starts to decompose
Oh wouldn't it be funny
If you didn't have a nose?

Where would we be without our hooters?
Nothing else would really suit us.
And think of those who
Rub their noses
Life would be tough for
Eskimoses

You couldn't wear your glasses
If you didn't have a nose
And what would bullies aim for
When it came to blows?
Where would nostrils be without them?
When it's runny how it glows
Oh wouldn't it be funny
If you didn't have a . . .

        have a . . .

        have a . . .

                a . . .

                a . . . choo!

Reward and Punishment

If you are good I will give you:

A pillow of blue strawberries
A swimming pool of Häagen-Dazs
A mirror of imagination
A pocketful of yes's
A hiss of sleigh rides
A lunch box of swirling planets

If you are very good I will give you:

A doorway of happy endings
A hedgerow of diamonds
A surfboard of dolphins
A cat's paw of tickles
A carton of fresh rainbow-juice
A forest of chocolate wardrobes

But if you are naughty you will get:

A burst of balloon
A screech of wolf
A hoof of piggy bank
A twitch of sideways
A splinter of thirst
A precipice of banana skins

If you are very naughty you will get:

A tyrannosaurus of broccoli
A rucksack of bony elbows
A skeleton of lost pencils
A flag of inconvenience
A chill of false laughter
A detention that lasts forever, and ever, and ev . . .

Take a Bow, Cow

Take a bow, cow.
You with the beautiful eyes.
Without you, there'd be no ice cream,
No Milky Way in the skies.
Without you, coffee and cocoa
Would be undrinkable.
Imagine a world without MOO?
Unthinkable.

Love a Duck

I love a duck called Jack
He's my very favourite pet
But last week he took poorly
So I took him to the vet.

The vet said: 'Lad, the news is bad
Your duck has lost its quack
And there's nowt veterinary science
Can do to bring it back.'

A quackless duck? What thankless luck!
Struck dumb without a word
Rendered mute like a bunged-up flute
My splendid tongue-tied bird.

*   *   *

All day now on the duvet
He sits and occasionally sighs
Dreaming of a miracle
A faraway look in his eyes.

Like an orphan for his mother
Like a maiden for her lover
Waiting silently is Jack
For the gab to come back

For the gift of tongues that goes . . .

QUACK!

Jellyfish Pie

Shuna chewed my tuna sandwich
Molly demolished my cucumber bap
Kylie slyly nibbled my bagel
Gavin unravelled my Mexican wrap

Betty bit my bacon butty
Gupta gulped my hard-boiled egg
Patsy pinched my crusty pasty
Nigella gnawed my chicken leg

Lisa licked my slice of pizza
Nicola nicked my shrimp on rye
Stephanie scoffed my stuffed panini
But nobody touched my jellyfish pie.

Stop, Thief!

There's something about the seaside
I don't understand

Who steals the footprints
We leave in the sand?

Pull the Other One

A crab, I am told,
   will not bite
or poison you
   just for spite.

Won't lie in wait
   beneath a stone
until one morning,
   out alone

You poke a finger
   like a fool
into an innocent-
   looking pool.

Won't leap out
   and grab your hand
drag you sideways
   o'er the sand

To the bottom
   of the sea
and eat you, dressed,
   for Sunday tea.

A crab, I am told,
   is a bundle of fun.
(With claws like that?
   Pull the other one!)

OUCH!

Seagulls

Seagulls are eagles
with no head for heights

For soggy old crusts
they get into fights

Out-of-tune buskers
beggars and screechers

Seagulls are not
my favourite creatures.

Aquarium

The ocean's out there
It's vast and it's home
And I want to be in it
With the freedom to roam

Not stuck in a prison
That's made out of glass
For humans to peer into
As they file past

It's all right for goldfish
And small fry like that
But I deserve more
Than being ogled at

Imagine the look
You'd have on your face
If you had to live
In such a small space

Little wonder
That I look so glum
Banged up in a seaside
Aquarium.

Teapet

A teapet
I can recommend
to those who need
a loyal friend

Quiet, reliable
he'll never stray
content to sit
on his kitchen tray

Give him water
stroke his spout
say 'Thank you'
when the tea comes out.

The Tofu-Eating Tiger

If a tiger invites you round for tea
and offers you tofu,
you can take it from me
he's only pretending.

It's merely a ploy
to fool an innocent girl or boy
into thinking he's sweet.
A vegetarian tiger who doesn't eat meat.

Rubbish! Just look at those jaws.
Were they designed for chewing rice?
And those claws. For peeling bananas?
Take my advice:

Stay calm. Be polite.
Eat up your tofu and ask for more.
When the feline is in the kitchen
make a beeline for the door.

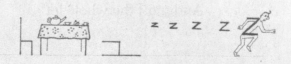

The Kleptomaniac

(klepto — from the Greek word kleptes, *meaning thief)*

Beware the Kleptomaniac
Who knows not wrong from right
He'll wait until you turn your back
Then steal everything in sight:

The nose from a snowman
(Be it carrot or coal)

The stick from a blindman
From the beggar his bowl

The smoke from a chimney
The leaves from a tree

A kitten's miaow
(Pretty mean you'll agree)

He'll pinch a used teabag
From out of the pot

A field of potatoes
And scoff the whole lot

(Is baby still there,
Asleep in its cot?)

He'll rob the baton
From a conductor on stage

All the books from the library
Page by page

He'll snaffle your shadow
As you bask in the sun

Pilfer the currants
From out of your bun

He'll lift the wind
Right out of your sails

Hold your hand
And make off with your nails

When he's around
Things just disappear

F nnily eno gh
I th nk th re's one ar und h re!

The All-Purpose Children's Poem

The first verse contains a princess
Two witches (one evil, one good)
There's a castle in it somewhere
And a dark, enchanted wood.

The second has ghosts and vampires
Monsters with foul-smelling breath
It sends shivers down the book spine
And scares everybody to death.

The third verse is one of my favourites
With rabbits in skirts and trousers
Who talk to each other like we do
And live in neat little houses.

The fourth is bang up to date
And in it anything goes
Set in the city, it doesn't rhyme
(Although, in a way it does).

The fifth verse is set in the future
(And, as you can see, it's the last)
When the Word was made Computer
And books are a thing of the past.

Bookworms

Bookworms are the cleverest
of all the worms I know

While others meet their fate
on a fisherman's hook as bait

Or churn out silk, guzzle soil
or simply burn and glow

They loll about in libraries
eating words to make them grow

In long-forgotten classics
Latin tracts and dusty tomes

Snug as bugs they hunker down
and set up family homes

Vegetarians mainly,
they are careful what they eat

Avoiding names of animals
or references to meat

They live to ripe old ages
and when it's time to wend

They slip between the pages
curl up, and eat 'The End'.

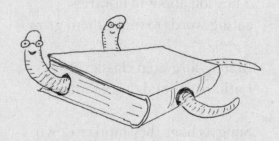

How to End a Poem

Knowing how to end a poem
is not as easy as people think.
It's not simply a matter
of putting in a full stop
and then adding your name.

My advice would be to count up to ten
and then shout, 'One more line
and then I'm coming, ready or not.'

Lost and Found

'Welcome to the Lost and Found
Step inside and look around

Enjoy the visit but take extra care
There's a boa constrictor loose somewhere

On buses and trains you wouldn't believe
The crazy things that passengers leave

A dodgem car, I kid you not
Hot-water bottle full, but no longer hot

Leopard-skin tights for the fuller figure
A pineapple carved with the face of Mick Jagger

Deflating slowly, a lead balloon
A barrel of monkeys and a red baboon

Bikes and skateboards by the score
Two steaming bags of horse manure

Rucksacks, tents and rolled-up beds
If they weren't screwed on they'd lose their heads

Stop for a moment, do I hear a strange hissing?
Let me just check there's nobody missing

No, all present and correct I'm glad to say
The snake has probably slithered away

Where was I? Oh yes, an electric chair,
Dozens of dolls and a huge teddy bear

A dodgy piano and a didgeridoo
A doddery dog and a portable loo

A ventriloquist's dummy at a loss for words
Three French hens and four calling birds

What's that noise? A strangling sound?
It's the giant snake. Don't turn around

Run for your lives, and I'm sorry to say
We're definitely closed for the rest of the day.'

The Feather Boa Constrictor

The feather boa constrictor
It's no joke.

It tickles as it tightens

You burst out laughing
Then you choke.

Digeridoo

Catfish
take catnaps on seabeds
Sticklebacks
stick like glue
Terrapins
are terrific with needles
But what does a didgery do?

Bloodhounds
play good rounds of poker
Chihuahuas
do nothing but chew
Poodles
make puddles to paddle in
But what does a didgery do?

A puffin
will stuff in a muffin
A canary
can nearly canoe
Humming-birds
hum something rotten
But what does a didgery do?

Tapeworms
play tapes while out jogging
Flies
feed for free at the zoo
Headlice
use headlights at night-time
But what does a didgery do?

What does a didgery
What does a didgery
What does a didgery do?

Fruit Bats

Fruit bats come in all shapes and sizes
banana-shaped
pear-shaped
they're full of surprises

Huge watermelon
and grapefruit bats
Cherry bats and plum bats
Lychees and kumquats

Hanging in the belfry
is that a satsuma?
Another example
of crazy bats' humour?

You think that's a strawberry
glowing on a bush?
You go to pick it and *whoosh*
What a fright!

As arrowing, shrieking
it takes flight
into the bottomless
Fruit bowl of night.

The Brushbaby

The Brushbaby
lives under the stairs
on a diet of dust
and old dog hairs

In darkness, dreading
the daily chores
of scrubbing steps
and kitchen floors

Doomed to an endless
life of grime
My poor little wooden
porcupine.

An Ass

Never harass an ass
An ass will never forgive
Compared to an ass, an elephant
Has a memory like a sieve.

For months, maybe years off,
When you've forgotten what you said
He'll burst into your bedroom
And turf you out of bed.

He'll bite your nose and ears off
He'll trample on your head
As you bleed, and plead for mercy,
And you've forgotten what you said.

* * *

'Not true! Not true!' I hear you cry,
'The ass is the apple of our Lord's eye.'
A sweet old donkey? Perhaps you're right.
(But lock your bedroom door each night!)

5 Ways to Stop Grizzly Bears from Spoiling Your Picnic

1) Shoo them away.

2) Lend them your teddy bears to play with.

3) Have food that Grizzly Bears don't like
(e.g. Fish heads . . . Donkey drops . . .
Rat toenails . . . Frog eyes . . . Pig whiskers . . .
Baboon bellybuttons . . . Bat milk . . .).
Definitely NOT Honey!

4) Have the picnic in a country where
there aren't any Grizzly Bears:
South America for instance.
(But watch out for tarantulas, crocodiles, boa
constrictors, giant hamsters and child-eating
goldfish!)

5) Learn a few Grizzly Bear phrases like:

'Grrr'	('Good afternoon.')
'Grra Grra'	('I'm sorry, but this is a private picnic.')
'GURRR GURRR'	('Scram, or I shall call the armed militia.')

Ostrich

One evening
an ostrich
buried his head
in the sand
and fell asleep

On waking
he couldn't remember
where he'd buried it.

Beware the Allivator

at the top.

then eat you

his back

ride upon

let you

he will

in a shop

see one

if you

allivator

Beware the

A Domesticated Donkey

A domesticated donkey from Slough
Wished to knit a new jumper but how?
 Attempts with her ears
 Resulted in tears
So, instead, she knitted her brow.

The Snowman

Mother, while you were at the shops
and I was snoozing in my chair
I heard a tap at the window
saw a snowman standing there

He looked so cold and miserable
I almost could have cried
so I put the kettle on
and invited him inside

I made him a cup of cocoa
to warm the cockles of his nose
then he snuggled in front of the fire
for a cosy little doze

He lay there warm and smiling
softly counting sheep
I eavesdropped for a little while
then I too fell asleep

Seems he awoke and tiptoed out
exactly when I'm not too sure
it's a wonder you didn't see him
as you came in through the door

(oh, and by the way,
the kitten's made a puddle on the floor)

The Kitten's First Spring

There's a robin
There's a bluebird
Tail a'bobbin
It's a new bird

There's a crocus
Puts in focus
My first spring.

There's a March hare
What a sprinter
Been in training
All through winter

Pussy willow
What a thrill, O
My first spring.

A day-old foal
Legs a jumble
Like he's on stilts
Takes a tumble

He shakes his mane
Then tries again
His first spring.

See the hedgerow
Smell the blossom
When the wind blows
It'll toss 'em

While daffodils
Embrace the hills
My first spring.

Count the cowslips
Hear the bluebells
All the colours
All the new smells

Just a daisy
Can amaze me
My first spring.

A Meerkat Lullaby

Hush, pretty meerkitten, don't you cry
Mummy will sing you a lullaby
Daddy on guard is standing near
Ready to bark should danger appear

His back is straight, his hindlegs long
His hearing acute, his eyesight strong
So go to sleep my little beauty
Safe with Daddy on sentry duty.

Old Hippos

Old hippos
   one supposes
have terrible
   colds in the noses

Attracted to these
   nasal saunas
germs build their nests
   in darkest corners

Then hang a sign
   that says politely
(streaming, streaming,
   day and nightly)

'Thank you for havin' us
in your nostrils so cavernous.'

I've Got a Cold

I've got a cold
And it's not funny

My throat is numb
My nose is runny

My ears are burning
My fingers are itching

My teeth are wobbly
My eyebrows are twitching

My kneecaps have slipped
My bottom's like jelly

The button's come off
My silly old belly

My chin has doubled
My toes are twisted

My ankles have swollen
My elbows are blistered

My back is all spotty
My hair's turning white

I sneeze through the day
And cough through the night

I've got a cold
And I'm going insane

(Apart from all that
I'm as right as rain).

No Room to Swing a Cat

My room is very, very small
The bed is up against the wall
Ceiling too low to toss a ball

Whenever Grandad pays a call
(Although he's old, he's very tall)
On bony knees he has to crawl

The smile on the cat says it all:
No room to swing me, room's too small.

Mafia Cats

We're the Mafia cats
   Bugsy, Franco and Toni
We're crazy for pizza
   With hot pepperoni

We run all the rackets
   From gambling to vice
On St Valentine's Day
   We massacre mice

We always wear shades
   To show that we're meanies
Big hats and sharp suits
   And drive Lamborghinis

We're the Mafia cats
   Bugsy, Franco and Toni
Love Sicilian wine
   And cheese macaroni

But we have a secret
   (And if you dare tell
You'll end up with the kitten
   At the bottom of the well

Or covered in concrete
    And thrown into the deep
For this is one secret
    You really must keep).

We're the Cosa Nostra
    Run the scams and the fiddles
But at home we are
    Mopsy, Ginger and Tiddles.

Cool Cat

My cat may look like your cat
With know-it-all eyes like yours
Spreadeagling itself on your tummy
To practise sharpening its claws

My cat may look like your cat
With sticky-out whiskers like yours
And the knack of slipping off branches
To land safely each time on all-paws

My cat may sound like your cat
With a pitiful mew like yours
After scratching the arms of the sofa
Tries to burrow under closed doors

My cat may look like your cat
And my cat may sound like yours
But my cat plays the saxophone
And dances to wild applause.

Cabbage

The cabbage is a funny veg.
All crisp, and green, and brainy.
I sometimes wear one on my head
When it's cold and rainy.

The Rolling Meatball

I was eating spaghetti
It tasted just great
When one of the meatballs
Jumped off the plate

Before I could ask
My mother for more
It rolled through the kitchen
And out of the door

I tried to catch it
But I tried in vain
It rolled down the road
Fell into a drain

I rang the police
And the fire brigade
Who arrived with a net
A rope and a spade

They scooped it out
(It was covered in slime)
'Thanks,' I cried
And without wasting time

Hurried back home
Where the meatball, of course
I ate with a dollop
Of tomato sauce.

Rainbow Menu

(Durban, South Africa)

Overlooking the harbour on the twentieth floor
Breakfasting on food I've never tasted before

The fun is in mixing the exotic and unknown
With stuff that I'm familiar with at home

Streaky back bacon with banana, lightly grilled
Pork sausages with pawpaw and mango, slightly chilled

Smoked salmon slices with sweet pickled figs
Biltong with guava and scrambled eggs

Calamari, pineapple and I suppose a
Strawberry yoghurt goes well with samosa

If the waiters think me mad they don't let it show
'Another kipper with your kiwi fruit, sir? Just let
   me know.'

Biryani, salami and butternut squash
My platter a palette of multicoloured nosh

Lucky the poet composing this oration
On a rainbow menu in a rainbow nation.

Good Enough to Eat

This poem looks scrumptious
This poem looks great
I wish I had a poem like this
Each morning on my plate

This poem looks tasty
This poem looks sweet
And if it's good enough to read
Then it's good enough to eat

Just Desserts

Jelly and custard, lemon meringue pie
Sherry trifle with cream piled high

Mincemeat tart and blackberry sponge
Roly-poly with syrupy gunge

Chocolate-coated profiterole
Sugary doughnut (without the hole)

Pineapple fritters and crème brûlée
Treacle toffee straight from the tray

Ice cream with banana split in two
Butterscotch fudge, sticky like glue

Rhubarb crumble and strawberry cheesecake
Brandy snaps that'll make your teeth ache

Christmas pudding, just one more slice
For goodness' sake, take my advice:

If all you eat is just desserts
One day you'll get your just desserts.

A Weak Poem

(To be read lying down)

Oh dear, this poem is very weak

It can hardly stand up straight

Which comes from eating junk food

And going to bed too late.

A Llama

Tick tock, tick tock
The llama farmer
winding his flock

Tick tock, tick tock
Setting his
a llama clock.

Downhill Racer

Down
    the
        snow
           white
        page
   we
slide.
    From
        side
           to
                side
           we
        glide.
           Pass
             obstacles
                with
                  ease.
                Words
             on
        skis.
Look out.
        Here
          comes
        a
      poem
        in
        a
           hurry!

Uphill Climb

<pre>
                          W
        Three   h
        Two   e
        One   e
        go.   e
        another   e
        have   e
        to   e
        top
        the
        to
        back
        way
        the
        all
        climb
        the
        is
        part
        boring
        only
        The
</pre>

The Midnight Skaters

It is midnight in the ice rink
    And all is cool and still.
Darkness seems to hold its breath
    Nothing moves, until

Out of the kitchen, one by one,
    The cutlery comes creeping,
Quiet as mice to the brink of the ice
    While all the world is sleeping.

Then suddenly, a serving spoon
    Switches on the light,
And the silver swoops upon the ice
    Screaming with delight.

The knives are high-speed skaters
    Round and round they race,
Blades hissing, sissing,
    Whizzing at a dizzy pace.

Forks twirl like dancers
    Pirouetting on the spot.
Teaspoons (who take no chances)
    Hold hands and giggle a lot.

All night long the fun goes on
    Until the sun, their friend,
Gives the warning signal
    That all good things must end.

So they slink back to the darkness
    Of the kitchen cutlery drawer
And steel themselves to wait
    Until it's time to skate once more.

At eight the canteen ladies
    Breeze in as good as gold
To lay the tables and wonder
    Why the cutlery is so cold.

The Nutcracker

I'm a nutcracker
no ifs or buts
My job is simple
I crack nuts

The bigger the better
the longer the fatter
The harder they come
the louder they shatter

Walnuts with attitude
the tightest of fits
I squeeze the trigger
and blow them to bits

Brazils take to the hills
pecans grow pale
Nuts shake in their shells
When I'm on their trail

A faceless gunslinger
I ride into town
Cashew! Cashew!
They all fall down.

Mr Pollard

In the dead of last night
we had a visit from Mr Pollard.
With his giant scissors
he lopped the branches off the trees in our road.

Today, like teenagers with bad haircuts,
they stand, gawky and embarrassed.
Birds stay clear. The sun bides its time.

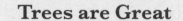

Trees are Great

Trees are great, they just stand and wait
They don't cry when they're teased
They don't eat much and they seldom shout
Trees are easily pleased

Trees are great, they like to congregate
For meetings in the park
They dance and sway, they stay all day
And talk till well after dark

Trees are great, they accept their fate
When it's pouring down with rain
They don't wear macs, it runs off their backs
But you never hear them complain

So answer me, please, if there weren't any trees
Where would children learn to climb?
Where would lovers carve their names?
Where would little birds nest?
Where would we hang the leaves?
Where would wood be?

Why Trees Have Got It All Wrong

Trees have got it all wrong
because they shed their leaves
as soon as it gets cold.

If they had any sense
they'd take them off in June
and let the scented breezes

whiffle through the branches
cooling the bare torso.
In high summer, more so.

*   *   *

Come autumn (not the fall)
they'd put on a new coat:
thick leaves, waxed and fur-lined

To keep them warm as toast,
whatever the weather.
Trees, get it together!

Animals with Long Ears

Animals with long ears
  Can hear every little sound:
A butterfly on tiptoe
  Snow settling on the ground

A rose blinking in the sunlight
  The last breath of a bee
The heartbeat of an egg
  Leaves taking leave of the tree

The shimmy of a golden carp
  The hiatus of a hawk
The wriggle of a baited worm
  The bobbing of a cork

The echo in a coral reef
  The moon urging the tide
A cloud changing shape
  They listen, open-eyed.

Animals with long ears
  Hear such sounds every day
And try to recapture
  In a melodious way

The music that surrounds them
So isn't it sad to say
That being tone-deaf their chorus
Is an ear-crunching BRAY.

Joy at the Sound

Joy at the silver birch in the morning sunshine
Joy at the bounce of the squirrel's tail

Joy at the swirl of cold milk in the blue bowl
Joy at the blink of its bubbles

Joy at the cat revving up on the lawn
Joy at the frogs that leapfrog to freedom

Joy at the screen as it fizzes to life
Joy at The Simpsons, Lisa and Bart

Joy at the dentist: 'Fine, see you next year'
Joy at the school gates: 'Closed'

Joy at the silver withholding the chocolate
Joy at the poem, two verses to go

Joy at the zing of the strings of the racquet
Joy at the bounce of the bright yellow ball

Joy at the key unlocking the door
Joy at the sound of your voice in the hall.

The Sound Collector

A stranger called this morning
Dressed all in black and grey
Put every sound into a bag
And carried them away

The whistling of the kettle
The turning of the lock
The purring of the kitten
The ticking of the clock

The popping of the toaster
The crunching of the flakes
When you spread the marmalade
The scraping noise it makes

The hissing of the frying pan
The ticking of the grill
The bubbling of the bathtub
As it starts to fill

The drumming of the raindrops
On the windowpane
When you do the washing-up
The gurgle of the drain

The crying of the baby
The squeaking of the chair
The swishing of the curtain
The creaking on the stair

A stranger called this morning
He didn't leave his name
Left us only silence
Life will never be the same.

My Brilliant Friend

He's brilliant at karate
He's brilliant at darts
He's brilliant at acting
He gets all the best parts

He's brilliant at swimming
He's brilliant at skates
He's brilliant at juggling
With real china plates

He's brilliant at poetry
He's brilliant at rhyme
He's brilliant at lessons
He comes top every time

He's Brilliant just Brilliant
With a capital B
(Although he's only average
In comparison with me).

Imaginary Friend

I've got a friend
no one can see
That nobody hears
only me

He's not a ghost
or anything scary
A cartoon rabbit
or a wicked fairy

He's hard to describe
(looks a bit like me)
Though bigger and stronger
like I want to be

He's there each morning
and throughout the day
We watch telly together
read or play

There are jokes to tell
and secrets to share
When I'm not well
it's good that he's there

We seldom argue
we never fight
(Because I'm the one
who's always right)

I know he's not real
it's only pretend
And I'll grow out of him
in the end

For when I'm older
I intend
To find an
un-imaginary friend.

Bubble Trouble

The trouble with Bobby is bubbles
Been his hobby since he was a boy
When Santa brought him a bubble
One Christmas instead of a toy

Since then he has tried to recapture
The magic of that shimmering sphere
And decided the blowing of bubbles
Would be his chosen career

Fairy Liquid he pours on his cornflakes
Scented soap he spreads on his toast
To be undisputed world champion
'A billion I'll blow!' his proud boast

Golden globes, silver orbs and Belishas
All manner of ball he creates
And with a fair wind behind him
A small zeppelin our hero inflates

But the trouble with all of his bubbles
Though perfect in every way
Though fashioned with love and attention
(And we're talking a thousand a day)

These incandescent flotillas
These gravitational blips
These would-be orbiting planets
Within seconds of leaving his lips

Go *POP!* Just like that

The Tongue-twister

Watch out for the dreaded Tongue-twister
When he pulls on his surgical gloves.
Keep your eyes open, your mouth tightly shut,
Twisting tongues is the thing that he loves.

It's the slippery, squirmy feel of them
As they wriggle like landed fish.
When he pulls and tugs and grapples
You'll gasp and gargle and wish

That you'd never pulled tongues at teacher
Or a stranger behind their back,
As he twists out your tongue and pops it
Into his bobbling, twisted-tongue sack.

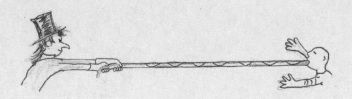

M. Barra-Sing

Sir asks a question
you really should know
You give the wrong answer
three times in a row
Who's the one who points the finger?
M. Barra-Sing

Texting coolly
down the street
You drop your mobile
at your feet
Who's the one who starts the laughter?
M. Barra-Sing

The deejay plays
your favourite track
You get up to dance
fall flat on your back
Who's the one you'd like to strangle?
M. Barra-Sing

Who makes you blush
from ear to ear?
Who makes you want
to disappear?
Who's to blame for everything?
M. Barra-Sing.

The Going Pains

Before I could even understand
The meaning of the word 'command'
I've had them. The going pains.

Go to your room
Go to bed
Go to sleep

Twinges that warned of trouble in store
And once in the classroom, the more
I felt them. The going pains.

Go to the back
Go and start again
Go to the Headmaster

From year to year I hear it grow
The unrelenting list of GO.
That bossy word that rhymes with NO
Still can hurt. The going pains.

Go
Go now
Why don't you just go.

A Poem Just for Me

Where am I now when I need me
Suddenly where have I gone
I'm so alone here without me
Tell me please what have I done?

Once I did most things together
I went for walks hand in hand
I shared my life so completely
I met my every demand.

Tell me I'll come back tomorrow
I'll keep my arms open wide
Tell me that I'll never leave me
My place is here at my side.

Maybe I've simply mislaid me
Like an umbrella or key
So until the day that I come my way
Here is a poem just for me.

Emus

To amuse
emus
on warm summer nights

Kiwis
do wiwis
from spectacular heights.

Bee's Knees

Ever seen a bee slip?
Ever kissed a bee's lip?

Ever felt a bee slap?
Ever sat on a bee's lap?

Ever made a bee start?
Ever eaten bee's tart?
    (rose petals and honey)

Ever told a bee 'Stop!'
Ever spun a bee's top?

Ever heard a bee sneeze?
Ever tickled bee's knees?

Nor me.

You Tell Me

When it takes a well-earned rest
Is it still a busy bee?

When a woodcutter chops it down
Is it still a tree?

Do ships wrecked on rugged rocks
Ever forgive the sea?

If it makes them smooth and soft
Would you rub your hands with Glee?

Questions, questions, questions
I've no idea, you tell me.

If you met a tiger in the woods
Would you invite it home for tea?

Would you cuddle a triceratops
Or scream out loud and flee?

Do locks at the end of a boring day
Look forward to the key?

If you found a rattlesnake in a baby's cot
Would you shake it or set it free?

Questions, questions, questions
I give in. You tell me.

Simple Questions

Is a well-wisher someone
Who wishes at a well?
Is a bad speller one
Who casts a wicked spell?

Is a pop singer someone
Who sings and then pops?
Is a shoplifter a giant
Who goes round lifting shops?

Is a night nurse a nurse
Who looks after the night?
Who puts it to bed
And then turns out the light?

Is a potholer a gunman
Who shoots holes in pots?
Does a babysitter really
Sit on tiny tots?

Does a pony trap
Trap ponies going to the fair?
Is fire-hose stockings
That firemen wear?

Is a fly fisherman an angler
Who fishes for flies?
Is an eye-opener a gadget
For opening eyes?

Is a light bulb a bulb
That is light as a feather?
Does an opera buff sing
In the altogether?

Does a lightning conductor
Conduct orchestras fast?
Is a past master a master
Who has mastered the past?

Is a scratch team so itchy
It scratches?
When a bricklayer lays a brick
What hatches?

Is a waiting room a room
That patiently waits?
Is a gatekeeper's hobby
Collecting gates?

Is a prayer mat a carpet
That sings hymns and prays?
Is a horsefly a fly
That gallops and neighs?

Will a pain killer kill you
In terrible pain?
Is a rain hood a gangsta
Who sings in the rain?

Is a card sharp a craftsman
Who sharpens cards?
Who guards women
When a guardsman guards?

Is a tree surgeon a doctor
Who is made out of wood?
Is a blood donor pitta bread
Stuffed with blood?

Is a sickbed a bed
That is feeling unwell?
Is a crime wave a criminal's
Wave of farewell?

Is a bent copper a policeman
Who has gone round the bend?
Is the bottom line the line
On your bottom?

THE END

Words

Like birds
who dream of eggs
before laying them

Words
I try to weigh
before saying them.

Give and Take

I give you clean air
You give me poisonous gas.
I give you mountains
You give me quarries.

I give you pure snow
You give me acid rain.
I give you spring fountains
You give me toxic canals.

I give you a butterfly
You gave me a plastic bottle.
I give you a blackbird
You gave me a stealth bomber.

I give you abundance
You give me waste.
I give you one last chance
You give me excuse after excuse.

The Man Who Steals Dreams

Santa Claus has a brother
A fact few people know
He does not have a friendly face
Or a beard as white as snow

He does not climb down chimneys
Or ride in an open sleigh
He is not kind and giving
But cruelly takes away

He is not fond of children
Or grown-ups who are kind
And emptiness the only gift
That he will leave behind

He is wraith, he is silent
He is greyness of steam
And if you're sleeping well tonight
Then hang on to your dream

He is sour, he is stooping
His cynic's cloak is black
And if he takes your dream away
You never get it back

Dreams with happy endings
With ambition and joy
Are the ones that he seeks
To capture and destroy

So, if you don't believe in Santa
Or in anything at all
The chances are his brother
Has already paid a call.

Tomorrow Has Your Name On It

Tomorrow has your name on it
It's written up there in the sky
As you set out on a journey
In search of the How? and the Why?

Oh the people you'll meet
The bright and the mad
The sights to be seen
The fun to be had.

Oh the dreams that you'll dream
The chances you'll take
The prizes you'll win
The hands that you'll shake.

But don't let your dreams
Get too big for their boots
Don't hanker after the flimflam of fame
If you hunger for mere celebrity
You'll be drawn like a moth to the flame.

For having dreams is not enough;
You must get down and do your stuff.
Take the ready with the rough.
Ride the punches, and my hunch is
You'll succeed when life gets tough.

And it will.
Bullies will want to bully you
For that's what bullies do
And you'll feel small and miserable
(Don't worry, I would too).

Even Big Bad Wolves have nightmares,
One of the reasons they howl at the moon.
Being scared is Nature's medicine.
Not nice, but it's over soon.

There'll be days you're made to feel foolish
When your head seems made out of wood
When you blush, mumble and shuffle
Feel embarrassed and misunderstood.

Things will get lost or stolen
Life doesn't turn out as you'd planned
You get sick and then you get better –
What's gone wrong? You can't understand.

Take your time.
Sing your own songs and laugh out loud.
Weep, if you need to
But away from the crowd.

Disappointments will ebb and flow
Like the tide upon the shore
But an angry storm will quickly go
And the sun rise up once more.

Oh the dreams that you'll dream
The promises you'll make
The friends that you find
Whom you'll never forsake.

Oh the dreams that you'll dream
May the good ones come true.
Being young is an adventure
How I wish I were you.

Today is the tomorrow we worried about
Yesterday and all last night.
And as days go, as days they do.
It seemed to go all right.

So dream your dreams and journey
Be tomorrow foul or fine
So you can say at the end of it
'Amazing! Today was mine.'

As Young as You Feel

I'd be the first to swim the Channel in a tutu
The first to climb Mount Everest eating fire
The first to cross the vast Saharan desert
Barefoot on a tightrope of barbed wire.

I'd be the first to win the Ladies Open Doubles
At Wimbledon, at tennis, on my own
The first to catch a fierce and mighty dragon
Whose roar is now the ringtone on my phone.

I'd be the first to surf Down Under underwater
On the belly of a hammer-headed shark
Race an alligator up an escalator
Go camping with vampires after dark.

I'd be the first to skateboard to the South Pole
South polar bears all marvelling at my skill
The first to hang-glide all the way to Venus
And get back quick, because it's all downhill.

I'd be the first to leapfrog Blackpool Tower
Clear Grand Canyon in one almighty leap
Dream about the FA Cup at Wembley
Score the winning goal while walking in my sleep.

I'd be the first in all these things
So it's painful to reveal
That maybe now I'm far too old
(Though they say you're as young as you feel).

His tightrope act was floorless.

Index of First Lines

'Roger McGough is a true original and more than one generation would be much the poorer without him' – *The Times Educational Supplement*

'. . . A collection that works well on the page
and is a delight to read aloud' – *Guardian*

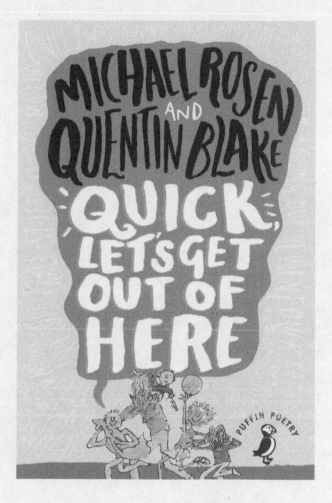

'Michael Rosen is one of our most popular writers
– the champion for every bored, overdrilled,
tested-to-tears pupil in the land' – *The Times*

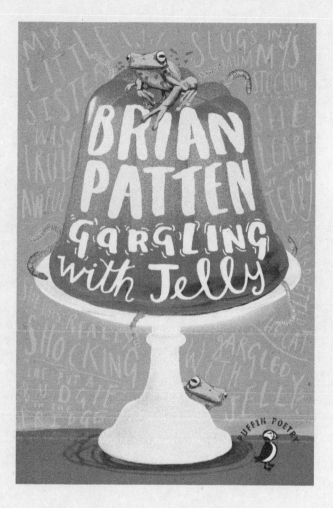

Full of Brian Patten's wonderful wit!

'Very silly, utterly crazy humour' – Jeremy Strong,
Guardian

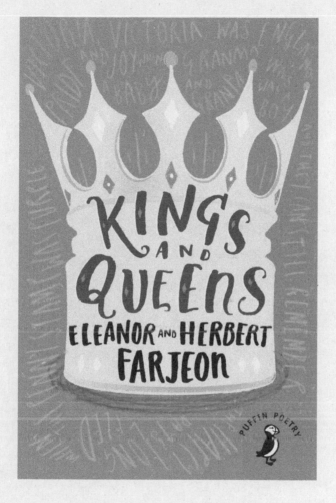

A collection of witty and brilliant poems that
bring our monarchy to life!

It all started with a Scarecrow

Puffin is over seventy years old.
Sounds ancient, doesn't it? But Puffin has never been
so lively. We're always on the lookout for the next big
idea, which is how it began all those years ago.

Penguin Books was a big idea from the mind of
a man called Allen Lane, who in 1935 invented
the quality paperback and changed the world.
**And from great Penguins, great Puffins grew,
changing the face of children's books forever.**

The first four Puffin Picture Books were hatched in 1940 and the
first Puffin story book featured a man with broomstick arms called
Worzel Gummidge. In 1967 Kaye Webb, Puffin Editor, started the
Puffin Club, promising to **'make children into readers'.**
She kept that promise and over 200,000 children became devoted
Puffineers through their quarterly instalments of *Puffin Post*.

Many years from now, we hope you'll look back and
remember Puffin with a smile. **No matter what your age
or what you're into, there's a Puffin for everyone.**
The possibilities are endless, but one thing is for sure:
whether it's a picture book or a paperback, a sticker book
or a hardback, **if it's got that little Puffin
on it – it's bound to be good.**

www.puffinbooks.com